1.5

Hello, Reader!

Think about all the stories you have read this year. Which character do you like best?

In this book, you will meet some children who make a new friend. You will also meet a hen that gets a surprise, two greedy bears that learn a lesson, and a toad with a good friend.

Read on to discover a world of Wonders.

HOUGHTON MIFFLIN
Reading

Wonders

Senior Authors
J. David Cooper
John J. Pikulski

Authors
Patricia A. Ackerman
Kathryn H. Au
David J. Chard
Gilbert G. Garcia
Claude N. Goldenberg
Marjorie Y. Lipson
Susan E. Page
Shane Templeton
Sheila W. Valencia
MaryEllen Vogt

Consultants
Linda H. Butler
Linnea C. Ehri
Carla B. Ford

HOUGHTON MIFFLIN
Reading
A Legacy of Literacy

 HOUGHTON MIFFLIN BOSTON • MORRIS PLAINS, NJ

California • Colorado • Georgia • Illinois • New Jersey • Texas

Cover and title page photography by Tony Scarpetta.

Cover illustration is from *Fireflies for Nathan,* by Shulamith Levey Oppenheim, illustrated by John Ward.
Text copyright © 1994 by Shulamith Levey Oppenheim. Illustrations copyright © 1994 by John Ward.
Reprinted by permission of HarperCollins Publishers. All rights reserved.

Acknowledgments begin on page 236.

Printed in the U.S.A.

ISBN: 0-618-25781-0

7 8 9 10 DW 11 10 09 08 07 06 05 04 03

Special Friends 12

Student Writing Model

Fussy Gail
by Anne Myers
illustrated by Kristina Stephenson

"Mama, can Gail eat lunch
with us?" asked Little Bear.
"She can if she knocks this
time!" smiled Mama Bear.

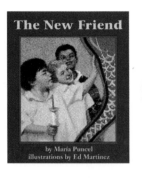

fiction

Phonics Library:
Jenny's Big Voice
Joy Boy
Shawn's Soy Sauce

Big Book

When I Was Little Like You

by Jill Paton Walsh
illustrated by
Stephen Lambert

On My Way Practice Readers

The Ant and the Dove

retold by
Mindy Menschell

Pen Pals

by Kathryn E. Lewis

Pet Shop

by Ryan Fadus

Theme Paperbacks

Mr. Santizo's Tasty Treats

by Alice K. Flanagan
photographs by
Romie Flanagan

Max Found Two Sticks

written and illustrated
by Brian Pinkney
CCBC "Choices"

Technology

Visit www.eduplace.com/kids **Education Place®**

Read at school Accelerated Reader®

Read at home www.bookadventure.org **Book Adventure**

Focus on

Folktales

We Can Do It! 138

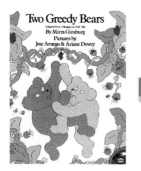

fantasy

Student Writing Model

Phonics Library:
Sport Gets a Bath
Home Run
Pet Store

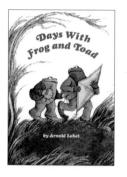

fantasy

Additional Resources

Big Book

I'll Catch the Moon
by Nina Crews
CCBC "Choices"

On My Way Practice Readers

You Can Help, Too!
by Kathryn E. Lewis

A Storm at the Farm
by Iris Littleman

Wind and Sun
retold by Nicolas Thilo

Theme Paperbacks

Bunny Cakes
written and illustrated by Rosemary Wells
IRA/CBC Children's Choice
NCTE Notable Children's Books in the Language Arts

Fireman Small
written and illustrated by Wong Herbert Yee
American Bookseller "Pick of the Lists"

Technology

Visit **www.eduplace.com/kids** **Education Place**®

Read at school **Accelerated Reader**®

Read at home **www.bookadventure.org** **Book Adventure**™

Special Friends

Read Together

The New Girl

I can feel
we're much the same,
though I don't
know your name.

What friends
we're going to be
when I know you
and you know me!

by Charlotte Zolotow

When I Am Old with You
Story by ANGELA JOHNSON Pictures by DAVID SOMAN

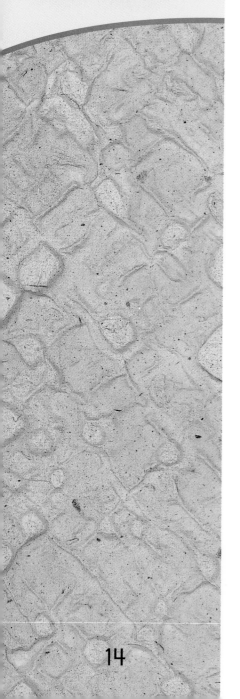

My Grandaddy

Read about the special things a grandfather and grandchild do in the next story.

Words to Know

around	though
dance	by
else	my
open	try
talk	cry
ever	any
ocean	Grandaddy

Practice Sentences

1. My Grandaddy likes to take walks by the ocean.
2. He likes to dance when no one else is around.
3. We try to talk every day.
4. Sometimes we're too busy to talk, though.
5. When I miss him, I start to cry.
6. Any day now, I will open my door and there he will be.
7. He is the best Grandaddy ever!

When I Am Old with You

Story by ANGELA JOHNSON   Pictures by DAVID SOMAN

 As you read the story, make sure you understand what is happening.

16

When I am old with you, Grandaddy,
I will sit in a big rocking chair beside
you and talk about everything.

An old dog will sit by my feet,
and I will swat flies all afternoon.

19

We'll go fishing too,
Grandaddy, down by that old pond
with the flat rocks all around.

We can fish beside the pond
or take that old canoe out.

We'll eat out of the picnic basket
all day and we won't catch any fish . . .
. . . but that's all right, Grandaddy.

When I am old with you, Grandaddy,
we will play cards all day underneath that
old tree by the road.

We'll drink cool water from a jug
and wave at all the cars that go by.

We'll play cards till the
lightning bugs shine in the trees . . .

. . . and we won't mind that we
forgot to keep score, Grandaddy.

When I am old with you, Grandaddy, we
will open up that old cedar chest and try on all
the old clothes that your grandaddy left you.

We can look at the old
pictures and try to imagine
the people in them.

It might make us cry . . .
but that's O.K.

29

30

In the mornings, Grandaddy, we will
cook bacon for breakfast and that's all.

We can eat it on the porch too.

In the evening we can roast corn on
a big fire and invite everyone we know to
come over and eat it. They'll all dance,
play cards, and talk about everything.

When I am old with you, Grandaddy,
we can take a trip to the ocean.

Have you ever seen the ocean,
Grandaddy?

We'll walk on the hot sand
and throw rocks at the waves.

We can wear big hats in the
afternoon like everyone else . . .
. . . and we'll sit in the water when
the day gets cool.

When our trip is over we will
follow the ocean as far as we can,
so we'll never forget it.

When I am old with you, Grandaddy,
we will get on the tractor and ride through
the fields of grass.

We will see the trees in the distance
and remember when this field was a forest.

We won't be sad though.

Grandaddy, when I am old with
you we will take long walks and speak
to all the people who walk by us.

We'll know them all, Grandaddy,
and they'll know us.

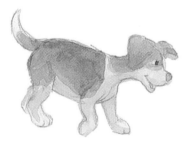

At the end of our walk, when we're tired,
Grandaddy, I will sit in a big rocking chair . . .
beside you.

Meet the Author and the Illustrator

Angela Johnson started writing in a diary when she was nine. Her advice for writers is to write your thoughts down so you can save them for later.

David Soman has always loved to draw and paint. When he was young, he liked to doodle. David Soman teaches art in New York City.

Internet

To find out more about Angela Johnson and David Soman, visit Education Place.

www.eduplace.com/kids

41

When I Am Old with You
Story by ANGELA JOHNSON Pictures by DAVID SOMAN

Think About the Story

1. Why do you think the grandchild and grandfather spend so much time together?

2. Do you think the grandchild will have happy memories of Grandaddy? Why?

3. What makes Grandaddy a special friend?

4. Which of the things in the story would you like to do with a friend? Why?

Internet

Post a Review

What did you think of this story?
Post your review at Education Place.

www.eduplace.com/kids

Let's Talk

Work with a partner. Choose a scene from the story. Act out a conversation that might happen between the grandchild and Grandaddy.

Take a Poll

In a group, take a poll about favorite activities from the story. Make a graph to show how many votes each activity gets.

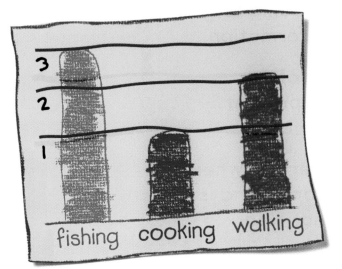

Expressing

Write a Message

Write a message to a special friend. Tell about something you could do together.

Tips

- **Think about things you both enjoy.**
- **Write clearly.**

Skill: Adjusting Your Reading Rate

- **Read more slowly** when you are reading to get information.

- **Look** for important details.

- **Reread** when something is not clear.

Inventions Then and Now

Bicycles

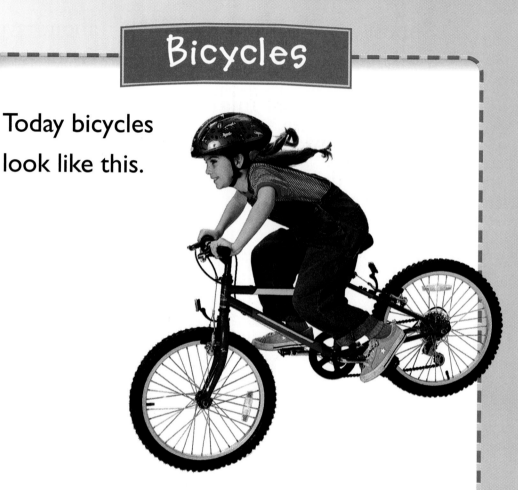

Today bicycles look like this.

In the past, bicycles didn't give a very smooth ride. Some people called these early bicycles boneshakers!

Telephones

Here are some of the telephones we use today. We can call people around the world.

The first telephone call was made from one room to another in the same building. Some early phones were made of wood and hung on walls.

Today clocks can look like these.

Before clocks were invented, some people used hourglasses. It takes one hour for the sand to run from the top bulb to the bottom bulb.

Past Inventions

Here are some other inventions from long ago. How are they different from the ones we use today?

lawn mower

phonograph

camera

roller skates

A Friendly Letter

A friendly letter tells a special friend about what you are doing. Use this student's writing as a model when you write a friendly letter of your own.

A friendly letter has the **date** and a **greeting**.

The main part of the letter is the **body**.

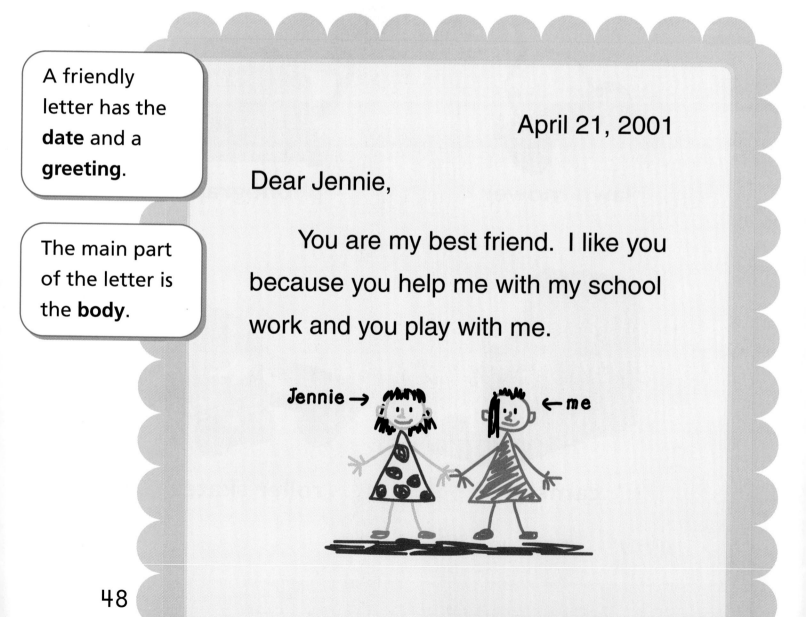

April 21, 2001

Dear Jennie,

You are my best friend. I like you because you help me with my school work and you play with me.

Jennie →   ← me

My favorite thing is when we pick flowers together. I am always happy to see you.

Your friend,
Marissa

Meet the Author

Marissa S.

Grade: one

State: Delaware

Hobbies: reading, writing, collecting rings

What she'd like to be when she grows up: a kindergarten teacher

49

The New Friend

by María Puncel
illustrations by Ed Martinez

A New Family

In the next story, you'll read about a new friend who moves to the neighborhood.

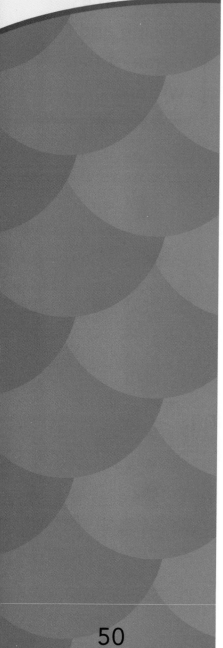

Words to Know

after	brushes
before	wishes
school	boxes
pretty	families
done	unloaded
buy	unpack
off	repaid
wash	

Practice Sentences

1. A new family came to buy the house next to our school.

2. They started to wash inside the house with brushes and mops.

3. They unloaded boxes off a truck and started to unpack.

4. They were done in no time.

5. After lunch, I took over a cake.

6. I gave them my best wishes.

7. Before long, the new family repaid us with some pretty flowers.

8. I hope our families will be friends!

Read Together

Meet the Author and the Illustrator

María Puncel wrote this story in Spanish. She lives in Spain. She first told stories to her six younger brothers and sisters. Now she writes books and TV shows.

EL AMIGO NUEVO

DE MARÍA PUNCEL
ILUSTRACIONES DE ULISES WENSELL

Ed Martinez thinks it's exciting to paint outdoors. He lives in the country in a house that's three hundred years old!

Internet

Go to Education Place to find out more about María Puncel and Ed Martinez.

www.eduplace.com/kids

The New Friend

by María Puncel
illustrations by Ed Martinez

 After you read the story, think about whether the author did a good job of telling the story.

Martin, Luis, and I lived in the city. Next door was an old house. No one had lived there for a long time.

One day a work crew came with pails and brushes. They started to wash and paint the empty house.

After they were done, and the paint had dried, the house looked pretty and new.

The next day a big truck pulled up. It was full of crates and boxes. A crew unloaded the boxes off the truck. A new family would soon live there.

Today Luis went over to the house next door.
He met a boy called Makoto. Then we all
met Makoto. Makoto was seven years old —
just like us.

Before long, we found out that Makoto played soccer. He could keep running and running. He was good at learning things, too. He learned all of our names by the end of the game.

Soon Makoto's family was all moved in. We met his mother and father. They were glad that Makoto had made some new friends.

While Makoto's mother and father went to buy food, Makoto stayed and played with us.

When Makoto's mother and father rejoined us, Martin, Makoto, and I helped them carry the bags into the house.

Makoto said he would show us around
his house. Then we went up to look at
Makoto's room.

Makoto still had a lot of boxes to unpack. He had some nice toys and kites. He said that on the next windy day, we could bring his kites outside and fly them. He said I could fly a kite by myself.

Then we went outside to look at Makoto's pictures from Japan. He had them in a green book.

On the first page, we saw Makoto's old house in Japan. On the next page, we saw Makoto's family in Japan. The last page had pictures of Makoto's friends. They showed Makoto's seventh birthday party. Makoto said he wishes we could meet his old friends.

At the end of the day, Makoto's mother and father repaid us for helping — with cookies! We said "please" and "thank you" and ate up.

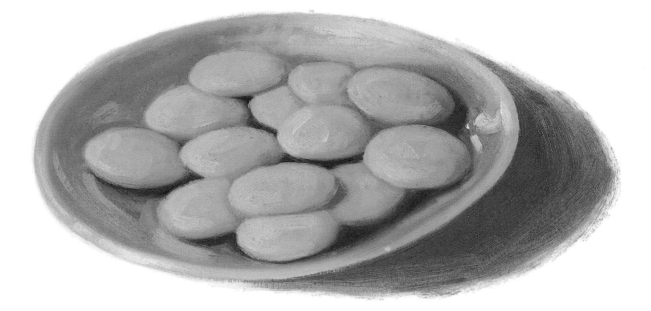

Makoto's father said he had a new job in the city. Makoto would be going to our school. We were all glad about that!

We said good-bye to Makoto and his mother and father. Then we went home to our families. We were glad to have a new friend next door.

Responding

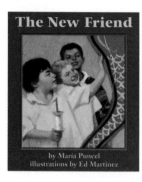

The New Friend

by María Puncel
illustrations by Ed Martínez

Think About the Story

1. How do you think the children felt about Makoto moving to their neighborhood?

2. How do you think Makoto felt about moving?

3. Do you think Makoto will like his new home? Why?

4. What would you do to make a new neighbor feel welcome?

Internet

Build a Story

Visit Education Place to put the story events in the order in which they happened.

www.eduplace.com/kids

Stay Healthy

Make a book about how to stay healthy. Write a sentence on each page and draw a picture to go with it.

Write an Invitation

Think of something you would like to do with a friend. Then send an invitation to your friend.

Tips
- **Begin with a greeting.**
- **Tell what you are inviting your friend to do.**
- **Include the date, time, and place.**

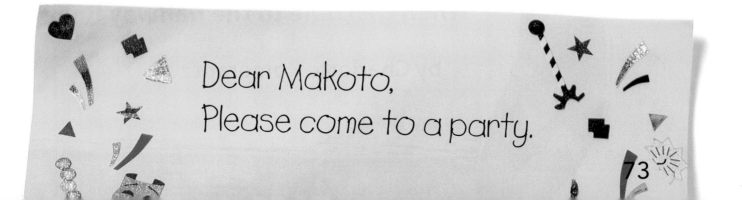

Dear Makoto,
Please come to a party.

Skill: How to
Read a Poem

- **Read** the poem aloud.

- **Listen** for the beat.

- **Reread** the poem and tap the beat.

I'll walk halfway to your house

if you walk halfway to mine.

We'll decide about the other half

when we come to the halfway line.

by Charlotte Pomerantz

HOPE

Sometimes when I'm lonely,
Don't know why,
Keep thinkin' I won't be lonely
By and by.

by Langston Hughes

Baby Birds

What happens when a hen doesn't get the kind of babies she expects? Read the next story to find out.

Words to Know

only	boy
together	pointed
watched	saw
baby	hawk
edge	taught
enough	fluffy
garden	fuzzy
sharp	

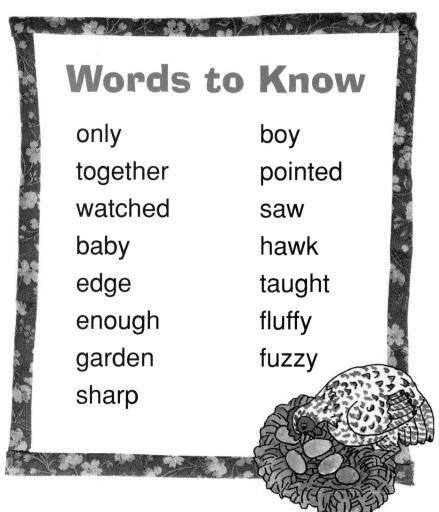

Practice Sentences

1. A boy and his mother went out together into the garden.
2. They saw fuzzy, fluffy baby birds on the ground.
3. They watched the birds creep to the edge of the garden.
4. The mother pointed up to a hawk with a sharp beak.
5. She taught the boy that the only safe place was in the nest.
6. "That should be enough to keep the baby birds safe," the mother said.

THE SURPRISE FAMILY

by LYNN REISER

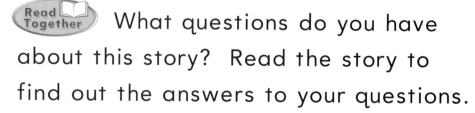

Read Together   What questions do you have about this story? Read the story to find out the answers to your questions.

First there was an egg.

One day it cracked open.

A baby chick looked out.
Nobody was there.
Where was her mother?

80

The baby chick looked up and saw —
a boy.

Her mother was a boy!
The boy was not the kind of mother
the chick had expected, but she loved
him anyway.

She followed him everywhere. The boy showed his baby chick how to find water and food and grit for her gizzard.

He taught her how to hide safe inside his jacket when a hawk flew by or when the vacuum cleaner came too close.

Every afternoon the boy and his baby
chick went for a walk around the garden.

At night she slept warm under the edge
of his quilt.

The baby chick grew and grew and became a little hen.

She still followed the boy everywhere, but now following the boy was not enough. She wanted a family to follow her.

She built a nest.

The boy found a clutch of eggs.
He gave them to the little hen.

She sat and warmed the eggs, and every
day she turned the eggs,

and she sat

and she sat

and she sat

and she sat

and she sat —

CRACK!

The eggs cracked open.
The babies looked out and saw
the little hen.

They followed her everywhere.
She showed them how to find water
and food and grit for their gizzards.

She taught them to run to her when she sang a danger song and danced a danger dance and to hide safe under her feathers.

Every afternoon the boy and the little
hen and the babies went for a walk
around the garden.

At night the babies slept warm under
the little hen's wings.

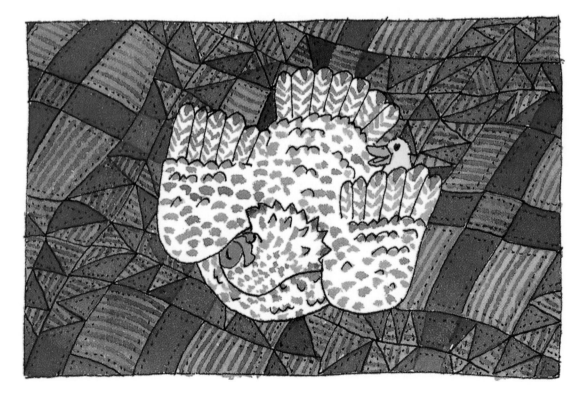

The little hen's family grew.
They still followed her everywhere,
but now walking around the garden
was not enough.
They wanted to walk by the pond.

So the boy and the hen took them to
walk by the pond.

They stood at the edge of the water.

They looked at the water.

They took a drink of the water.

They jumped into the water!

The little hen cried her DANGER cry —
her babies splashed.

The little hen danced her DANGER dance
— her babies swam.

The little hen held out her wings for her
babies to run under —
but they kept on swimming farther and
farther away.

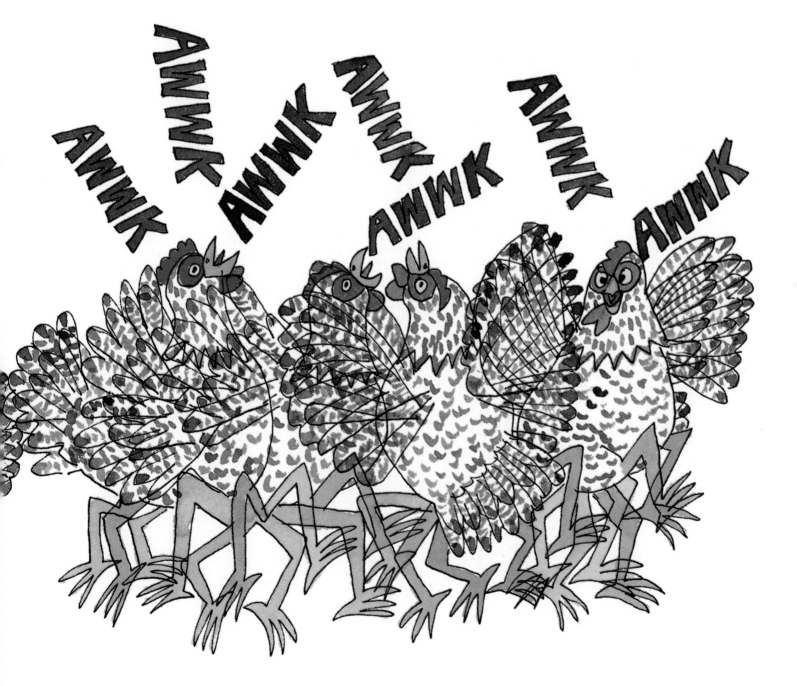

The little hen ran after them, but
when her feet got wet, she stopped.
She was a chicken.
Chickens cannot swim.

The little hen's babies swam out of sight.
Only her boy was left.

Then the little hen's babies turned around,
swam back, hopped out of the water,
flapped their wings, shook their tails,
and ran to their mother hen.

She gathered her babies in,
warm under her wings.
She looked at them.
They were safe.

She looked at them again.
Carefully.

Their beaks were not pointed like her
beak, or soft like her boy's mouth —
they were flat.

Their feet were not sharp like her feet,
or hard like her boy's shoes —
they were webbed.

Their feathers were not fluffy like her feathers, or fuzzy like her boy's jacket — they were waterproof.

Her babies did not look like chicks or like boys. They looked like ducklings.

Ducklings were not the kind of family she had expected, but she loved them anyway.

The ducklings grew and grew and became big ducks.

Some afternoons while the ducks swam in the pond, the boy walked around the garden, and the hen followed him.

Some afternoons while the ducks swam in the pond, the hen walked around the garden, and the boy followed her.

Other afternoons while the ducks swam in the pond, and the boy waded after them, the hen watched.

But every afternoon in the garden beside
the pond, after walking and swimming
and wading, there they all were, together,
under the little hen's wings.

QUACK

Meet the Author and Illustrator

Lynn Reiser not only writes children's books, but she is also a doctor and a professor. She thinks that all families are surprise families!

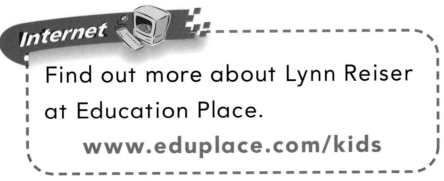

Find out more about Lynn Reiser at Education Place.

www.eduplace.com/kids

Think About the Story

1. Why do you think the story was called *The Surprise Family*?

2. How do you think the hen feels when her babies swim away in the pond?

3. Does it matter to the hen when she finds out her babies are different from her? Why?

4. What would you have done if you were the boy in the story?

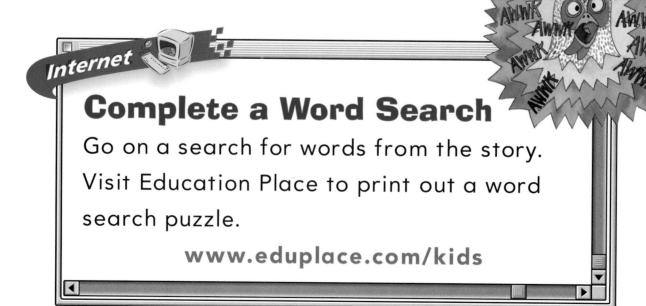

Internet

Complete a Word Search

Go on a search for words from the story. Visit Education Place to print out a word search puzzle.

www.eduplace.com/kids

Viewing

Words in Art

Look back at the story. Do you notice some words in the art? Find some other books that show words in the art. Share them with the group.

Science

Chicken and Duck

Draw a chicken and a duck. Label the parts of each animal that are different. Share your picture with the class.

Write a Newspaper Article

Write an article about what happens in *The Surprise Family*. Write sentences to tell the facts and include a picture.

Tip
- Write an interesting headline.

News of the Day

Hen's Babies Can Swim!

Skill: How to Read a Science Article

- **Read** the title of the article.

- **Read** the heading for each section.

- **Look** at the photos.

- **Predict** what you will learn.

- **Reread** if something is unclear.

Watch Them Grow

by Linda Martin

1. Hatching

A duckling pushes its way out of an egg laid by its mother.

2. Splash!

After only two days, a duckling goes for its first swim. It loves it!

3. New feathers

This duckling is not as round as it was before. Its baby feathers are falling out. New white feathers are growing in their place.

4. Fine wings

This duckling is six weeks old. All its feathers are white and its wings are big and strong. Soon it will fly for the first time.

Eggs

Some baby animals hatch from eggs. Do you think you can guess what will hatch from these eggs? Look for their mothers on the next page.

1

2

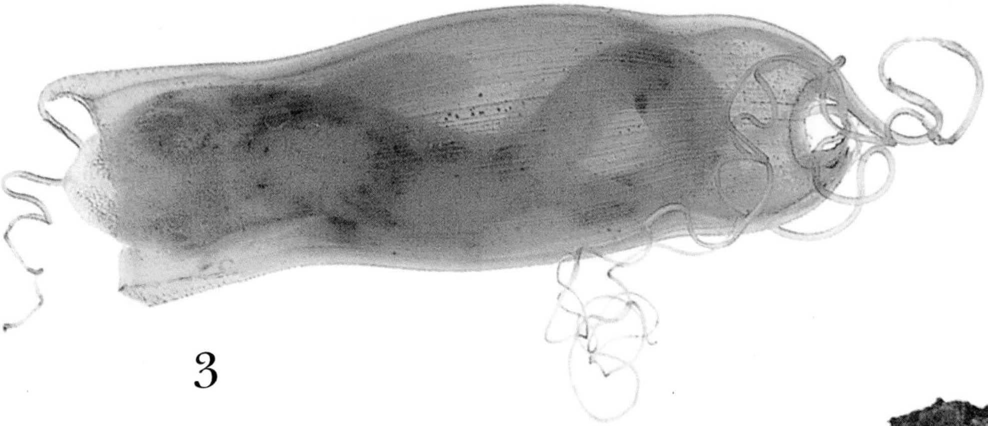

3

4

5

Spider

Duck

Owl

Dogfish

Lizard

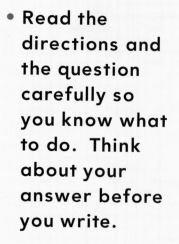
✔ Writing an Answer to a Question

Many tests ask you to write an answer to a question about something you have read. These questions need one or two sentences for the answer. Here is a sample test for *The Surprise Family*.

Tips

- Read the directions and the question carefully so you know what to do. Think about your answer before you write.

- Look back through the story if you need help.

In *The Surprise Family*, the hen and her babies are not alike in some ways. What are two things that are different about the hen and her babies? Write your answer.

Now look at a good answer one student wrote.

> The hen has a pointed beak and the babies have round beaks. The hen has sharp feet and the babies have webbed feet.

This answer is a good answer. It tells two things that are different about the hen and her babies.

I know that the hen and the babies had different kinds of beaks. I need to look at the story again to find one more thing.

Now that I know two things that are different about the hen and her babies, I'll write my answer.

Folktales

❁

What is a folktale?

- A folktale is a story that parents have told to their children, who then tell the same story to their children, and so on.

- Sometimes there are several folktales about the same character, such as Coyote or Anansi.

- Sometimes a character in a folktale learns a lesson.

Contents

Sister Hen's
Cool Drink

retold by Angela Shelf Medearis

One afternoon Hen went down by the
creek, looking for a cool drink.

Hen drank and drank. She did not hear
Crocodile as he came swimming up to her.

In a loud tone Crocodile said, "Stop
drinking from my creek, or I will eat you up!"
My, oh my! Hen ran from Crocodile as
fast as she could.

But Crocodile came slinking after her. He grabbed her tail.

"Please don't eat me, brother!" Hen said.

My, oh my! When Hen called Crocodile "brother," it made his jaws drop open. So, quick as a wink, Hen yanked her tail out and ran away. She did not stop running until she was safe in her nest.

"My, oh my!" Crocodile was thinking. "Why did Hen call me her brother?"

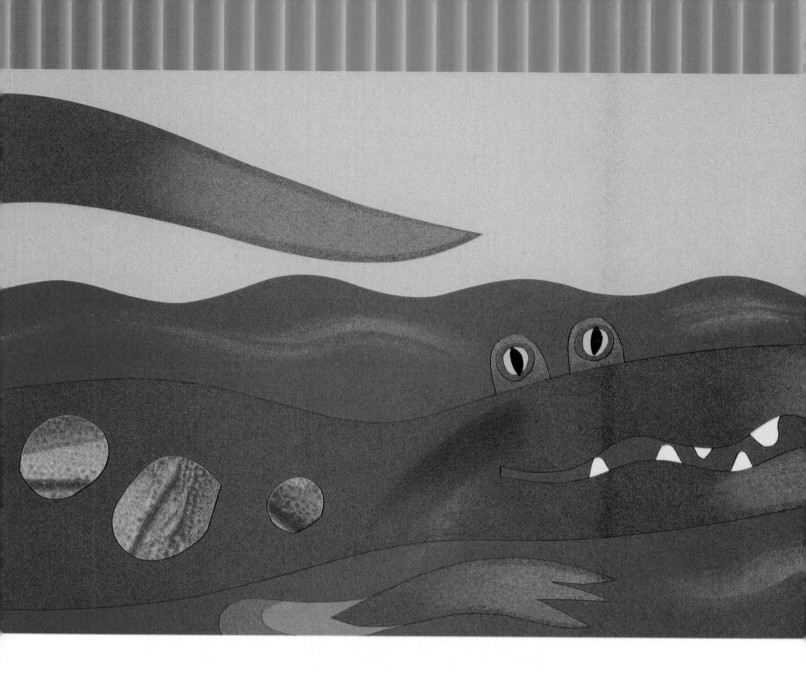

He slinked off the muddy bank into the
creek. Kaplunk!

Crocodile could not think why Hen
would call him "brother." He did not have
feet like Hen. Hen did not have teeth like
Crocodile.

He was still thinking about it the next day
when Hen came down from her nest for a cool
drink from the creek.

"Stop!" said Crocodile, slinking up next to
her. "I want to ask you something."

"What is it?" Hen said. This time she was
not afraid.

"Why did you call me your brother? I was thinking and thinking about it, but I do not get it," Crocodile said. "You are small and I am big. You are black and I am green. How can I be your brother?"

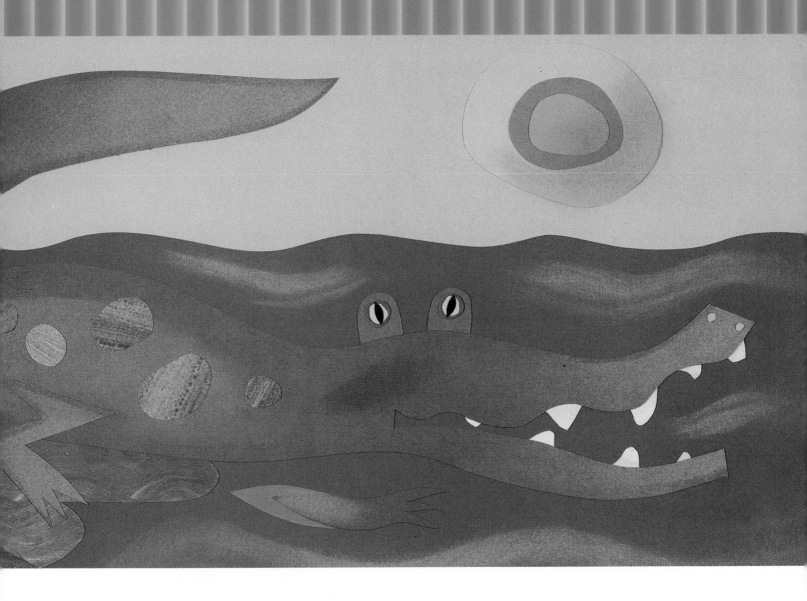

"Because," said Hen, "you come from an egg, and I come from an egg. So we must be family."

"Thank you," said Crocodile. "In that case, I guess I can't eat you after all."

Then Crocodile slinked off the muddy bank into the creek.

Kaplunk!

What Is in Mole's Sack?

retold by Gretchen Will Mayo

Coyote was walking along. "There is Mole's tunnel!" said Coyote.

He went over to look.

Scritch, scrape, scrape. Mole was busy.

"Working hard, Mole?" called Coyote.

"Yup!" Mole scraped some more.

Coyote found a tree and sat down to watch Mole. Coyote thought, "I'm so smart. I can rest in the shade. No hard work for me!"

Mole ran in and out of his house. He carried a little sack on his back.

"Mole, why are you working so hard?" Coyote called. He leaned against the tree.

"Busy cleaning," answered Mole. He scraped some more.

Coyote stared at Mole's sack. "Why is
Mole carrying that sack?" Coyote wondered.
"What does he have in it?"

Coyote called out, "Mole, you must have
something good in your sack."

"Nope," said Mole.

Coyote didn't believe him. Coyote thought, "If I had something good in a sack, I would keep it just for me. I'll bet Mole doesn't want to share."

Coyote called sweetly, "Let me look in your sack."

"Nope," said Mole.

"Just a little peek," begged Coyote. "I'll just open the sack a little bit."

"Don't," Mole said.

Coyote jumped up. He walked over to Mole. "I know. You want to keep the sack just for you."

"Nope," answered Mole.

"Well, I'm bigger," Coyote yelled at Mole. "You won't let me take a look, so I'll take the whole thing!"

And he did. Coyote grabbed Mole's sack and ran back down the road. He hid behind a rock. He smiled a little smile. Then he opened the sack.

"Eeeeeeeeee, no!" he cried. Zit-zit-zit-zit-zit! Out leaped a crowd of fleas. They jumped all over Coyote.

"Go away!" Coyote yelled. "Go away!" He slap-slap-slapped. He hopped. He rolled in the dirt. But the fleas hung on to Coyote. They liked his ears. They liked his back. They liked this big Coyote.

Coyote ran back to Mole's tunnel. "Mole!" he cried. "Take back your fleas. Take them back!"

But Mole ran away. He ran into his house and would not come out.

Coyote can't rest in the shade now. Scratch! Scratch! Scratch! Coyote is busy all the time. Scratching fleas is hard work.

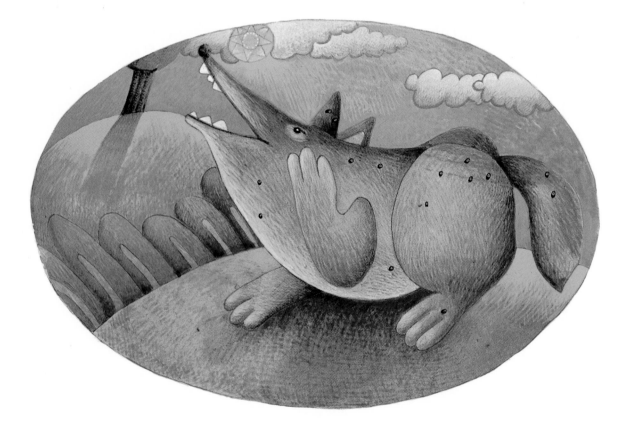

Write a Folktale

Would you like to write your own folktale? Here are some steps to follow:

1. Think of interesting characters for your folktale.

2. Decide if one character is going to learn a lesson.

3. Plan the order of events.

4. Think about adding dialogue and a funny twist at the end of your folktale.

Have a class folktale festival. Everyone can read aloud his or her folktale.

136

Other Folktales to Read

The Tortoise and the Hare

by Betty Miles (Aladdin)

Rabbit brags that he will win the race, but Tortoise comes in first.

The Cow in the House

by Harriet Ziefert (Puffin)

A man brings lots of noisy animals into his house to make it quieter.

The Three Little Pigs

by Betty Miles (Aladdin)

Three pigs outsmart a wolf who wants to eat them.

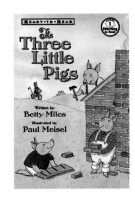

Once in a Wood: Ten Tales from Aesop

by Eve Rice (Greenwillow)

Ten easy fables by Aesop include "The Fox and the Crow."

We Can Do It!

Read Together

A Year Later

Last summer I couldn't
    swim at all;

I couldn't even float;

I had to use a rubber tube

Or hang on to a boat;

I had to sit on shore

While everybody swam;

But now it's this summer

And I can!

by Mary Ann Hoberman

139

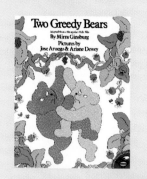

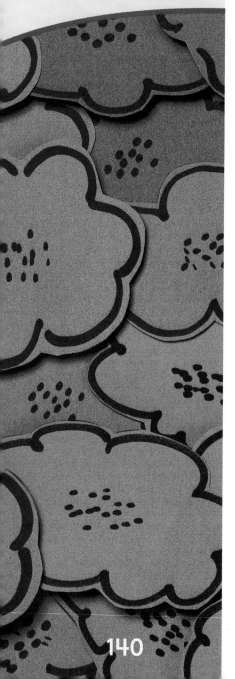

Thirsty Bears

Read the next story to find out what happens to two bear cubs who want the same piece of cheese. When a sly fox comes by, the bears learn a lesson!

Words to Know

began	burst
laugh	turning
sure	more
head	morning
divide	her
second	other
break	water
thirsty	better
thirstier	

Practice Sentences

1. One bear was thirsty.

2. The other bear was thirstier.

3. The second bear drank more and more water.

4. The first bear began to laugh.

5. "You are going to burst!" she said.

6. "You'd better stop drinking!"

7. Turning her head, the second bear said, "I am hungry."

8. "We can divide this food if we break it in two."

9. "Sure," said the first bear.

10. "We can do that in the morning."

Meet the Author

When she was young, **Mirra Ginsburg**'s parents taught her to love books. Now she is an author and has written more than 30 books. Some of her favorite things are folktales, poetry, and very old music.

Internet

Learn more about Mirra Ginsburg at Education Place.

www.eduplace.com/kids

Two Greedy Bears

Adapted from a Hungarian Folk Tale

By Mirra Ginsburg

Pictures by
Jose Aruego & Ariane Dewey

ALADDIN PICTURE BOOKS

Strategy Focus

 What do you think two greedy bear cubs will do when they find one piece of cheese? Read the story to find out.

Two bear cubs went out to see the world.
They walked and walked, till they came to a brook.
"I'm thirsty," said one.
"I'm thirstier," said the other.

They put their heads down to the water and drank.
"You had more," cried one, and drank some more.
"Now you had more," cried the other, and drank
some more.

And so they drank and drank, and their stomachs got bigger and bigger, till a frog peeked out of the water and laughed.

"Look at those pot-bellied bear cubs!
If they drink any more they'll burst!"

The bear cubs sat down on the grass and looked at their stomachs.

"I have a stomach ache," one cried.
"I have a bigger one," cried the other.
They cried and cried, till they fell asleep.

In the morning they woke up feeling better
and continued their journey.
"I am hungry," said one.
"I am hungrier," said the other.

And suddenly they saw a big round cheese
lying by the roadside. They wanted to
divide it. But they did not know how to
break it into equal parts. Each was afraid the
other would get the bigger piece.

They argued, and they growled, and they
began to fight, till a fox came by.

"What are you arguing about?" the sly one
asked the bear cubs.

"We don't know how to divide the cheese so
that we'll both get equal parts."

"That's easy," she said. "I'll help you."

She took the cheese and broke it in two.
But she made sure that one piece was bigger
than the other, and the bear cubs cried,
"That one is bigger!"

"Don't worry. I know what to do." And she
took a big bite out of the larger piece.
"Now that one's bigger!"

"Have patience!" And she took a bite out of
the second piece.
"Now this one's bigger!"

158

"Wait, wait," the fox said with her mouth full of cheese. "In just a moment they'll be equal." She took another bite, and then another.

160

And the bear cubs kept turning their black
noses from the bigger piece to the smaller
one, from the smaller one to the bigger one.
"Now this one's bigger!"
"Now that one's bigger!"

And the fox kept on dividing and dividing
the cheese, till she could eat no more.
"And now, good appetite to you, my friends!"
She flicked her tail and stalked away.

By then all that was left of the big round
cheese were two tiny crumbs.
But they were equal!

Meet the Illustrators
Jose Aruego and Ariane Dewey

Jose Aruego and Ariane Dewey are a team.
They have worked together on more than
65 books. Jose Aruego draws the lines,
and Ariane Dewey fills them in with color.

Internet

Learn more about Jose Aruego and
Ariane Dewey at Education Place.

www.eduplace.com/kids

Responding

Think About the Story

1. What did the two bears learn about solving problems?

2. What might the bears have done if the fox had not come by?

3. What would you do if you and a friend found one thing that you both wanted?

4. What advice would you give to the two greedy bears?

Internet

Post a Review

Write a review of *Two Greedy Bears*. Post your review at Education Place.

www.eduplace.com/kids

Divide It Up

1. Work with a partner. Draw a picture of something to share. Cut it out.

2. Decide how to divide your picture into two equal parts.

3. Cut the picture in two. Did you each get an equal piece?

Explaining

Write Sentences

Write some sentences to explain to a friend why they should share something with you.

Tips

- **Write the sentences as if you were speaking them.**
- **Use strong words that will convince your friend.**

Skill: How to Read a Cartoon

- **Notice** what is happening in the pictures.

- **Pay attention** to who is speaking before you read the words in the speech balloons.

Fraction Action

by Loreen Leedy

One morning, Miss Prime turned off all the lights in the classroom.

Watch how to draw a fraction.

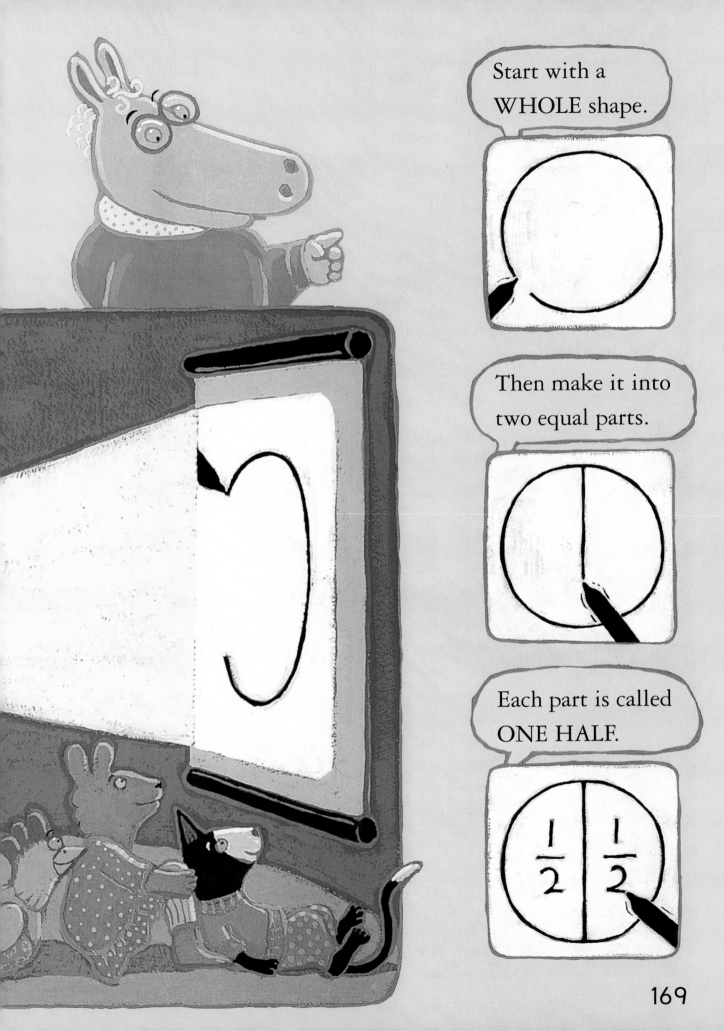

Start with a
WHOLE shape.

Then make it into
two equal parts.

Each part is called
ONE HALF.

$\frac{1}{2}$ $\frac{1}{2}$

169

Now let's think of some fractions in real life. Use your imagination to make a picture in your mind of what I say.

A tuna sandwich cut in HALF.

HALF a glass of juice.

A bowl of ice cream that is HALF vanilla and HALF chocolate.

171

Instructions

The reason for writing instructions is to tell others how to do or make something. Use this student's writing as a model when you write your own instructions.

How to Make a Bed

Do you want your bed to be messy or not? If you want your bed nice, then pay attention to my directions. First, you need the following materials:

It's important to list **materials** the reader will need.

1. Bed
2. Sheets
3. Pillow
4. Pillowcase
5. Blanket

Now follow the instructions in this order. First, put the sheets on the bed. (Hint, take the sheets and spread them out first.) Next, put the blankets on the bed. Then put the pillow on the bed. Fluff it. Finally, check it to see if the bed is messy or not.

Follow my directions, and your bed will look neat, too.

Present your steps in a clear **order**.

Use **time-order words** to show the reader what to do first, next, and last.

Meet the Author

Sara C.
Grade: one
State: Kentucky
Hobbies: reading, playing outdoors
What she'd like to be when she grows up: a veterinarian

A Jar of Fireflies

In this story, you will read about a boy who spends time with his grandparents. They catch fireflies in a jar just like the boy's father did when he was six.

Words to Know

above	minute
against	dark
already	star
caught	jar
begin	arm

Practice Sentences

1. Nathan got a jar to catch fireflies.

2. It was already dark when he saw the first star in the sky above.

3. Soon the fireflies would begin to come out.

4. Nathan saw a light against the dark sky.

5. He caught one firefly and put it in the jar.

6. In a minute, he had five fireflies in his jar.

7. He held the jar tight with his arm and let all the fireflies out.

Fireflies
FOR NATHAN

SHULAMITH LEVEY OPPENHEIM   pictures by JOHN WARD

Strategy Focus

Read Together   After you read, tell what the story was about.

Nathan asks, "When Daddy lived here, was he little like me?"

Nana smiles. "He was. We came here when he was almost six."

"I'm six already," Nathan says.

"You are," and Nana kisses Nathan on the cheek.

"What was Daddy's favorite thing to do when he was six?" Nathan asks.

Nana thinks and thinks. "Fireflies," she says.

"When night came on, the three of us — your poppy, too — would creep across the lawn just when the fireflies began to star the grass. Your daddy caught a few — three, four, or five. Enough to make a shining lamp. I know exactly where the jar has been."

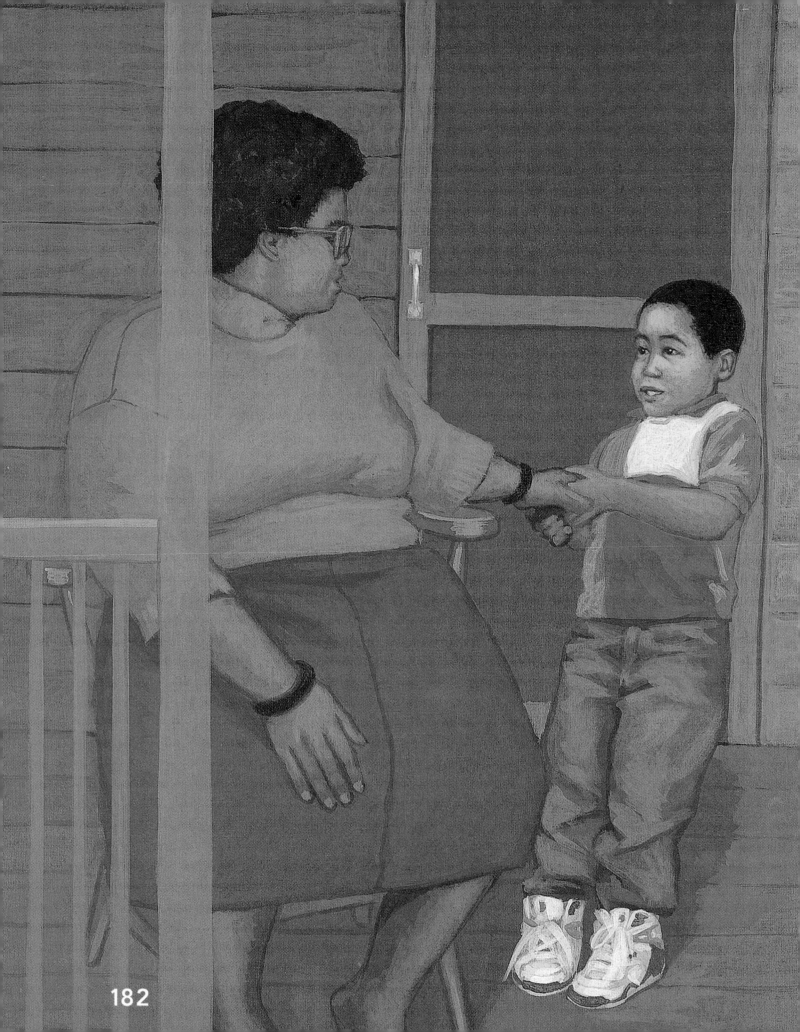

Nathan jumps up.

"Please, Nana, let's go in and get the jar.

It's almost night."

Nathan and Nana and Poppy are sitting in the grass. The sky is streaked with red. They're waiting for the night to come. Their feet are bare.

A ladybug begins a journey over Nathan's toes.
A goldfinch lights atop a spread of Queen Anne's
lace. A monarch butterfly wings in and out.
Deep in the pond the bullfrogs croak Good Night,
Good Night.

The minutes pass. Nathan shakes his leg. The ladybug falls off his foot. He tugs at Poppy's sleeve.

"Not yet," Poppy says.

More minutes pass. Nathan pulls at Nana's arm.

"It's getting dark. Where are the fireflies, Nana?"

"They'll be here soon."

Nana and Poppy nod their heads.

And *very* soon one, two, then three and four, the firefly glows appear. The blinking yellow lights are everywhere above the grass.

Nathan and Nana and Poppy creep across the lawn. "Slowly, slowly," Poppy whispers. "Let Nana hold the jar."

Nathan cups his hands around a glow.

"I've got one, Poppy! Nana, I want to see it blinking on and off."

"Careful," Nana warns.

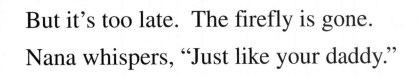

But it's too late. The firefly is gone.
Nana whispers, "Just like your daddy."

193

"You have to keep your hands cupped tightly till you drop the firefly in the jar."

Nathan promises, "I will," and soon the jar becomes a beacon in the night.

The firefly jar is sitting by the bed. Nana tucks the sheet up under Nathan's chin. Poppy kisses Nathan's cheek.

"Do you like catching fireflies with me?" Nathan asks.

"We do."

"Just as much as with my daddy?"

"Just as much."

"You can let them out when I'm asleep."

Nana and Poppy smile.

"That's what your daddy always said."

"I'm going to tell Mommy and Daddy all about catching fireflies with you."

Nathan yawns and lays the firefly jar beside him on the pillow. He presses his cheek against the glass.

"Nana, I'm glad you saved the jar."

"And so are we," Nana and Poppy tiptoe from the room. "And so are we."

Read Together

Meet the Author

Besides writing books, **Shulamith Levey Oppenheim** has acted in small plays. She writes books for children and adults. She gets story ideas from spending time with her five grandchildren.

Meet the Illustrator

John Ward is an artist who lives in New York. He learned about painting in art school. His illustrations of people and families have been in many children's books.

Internet

Visit Education Place to find out more about Shulamith Levey Oppenheim and John Ward.
www.eduplace.com/kids

Think About the Story

1. How is Nathan like his dad?

2. Why do you think Nathan's grandparents saved the firefly jar?

3. What do you think Nathan will tell his parents about his visit?

4. Would you like to visit Nathan's grandparents? Why?

Internet

E-mail a Friend

Did you enjoy reading *Fireflies for Nathan*? Send an e-mail to tell a friend about the story.

Glowing Pictures!

 Draw a scene from the story that shows fireflies.

 Use a pencil to poke holes through the fireflies on your paper.

 Shine a flashlight from behind your paper to make the fireflies glow!

Describing

Write a Character Sketch

Write a description about Nathan. Include details that will help someone else know what Nathan is like.

Tips

- List words that tell what Nathan looks like and how he acts.
- Include words from your list in the sentences that you write.

Poetry Link

Skill: How to Read a Poem

- **Read** the title.

- **Read** the poem aloud and listen for rhyming words.

- **Think about** what the poet is comparing in the poem.

The Firefly

On August nights
The firefly lights
Blink
ON and OFF
Amongst the trees
But have no need
For batteries.

by Douglas Florian

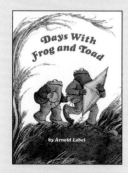

A Present for Toad

The next story is about a birthday present that's the wrong size. Discover how Frog makes the present fit.

Words to Know

able	smaller
eyes	larger
present	biggest
thoughts	

Practice Sentences

1. Frog wanted to get a present for Toad.

2. Frog had many thoughts — what if the present was a hat?

3. If the hat was smaller than Toad's head, it wouldn't fit.

4. If the hat was larger than Toad's head, it wouldn't fit.

5. If Frog got the biggest hat, it would cover Toad's eyes.

6. Would Frog be able to get the right present?

Meet the Author and Illustrator
Arnold Lobel

Growing up, Arnold Lobel read lots of books and drew many pictures. He became an illustrator and a writer. He created more than 70 children's books. Frog and Toad are his most famous characters. Arnold Lobel got the idea from toads his children played with in Vermont.

Internet

To find out more about Arnold Lobel, visit Education Place.

www.eduplace.com/kids

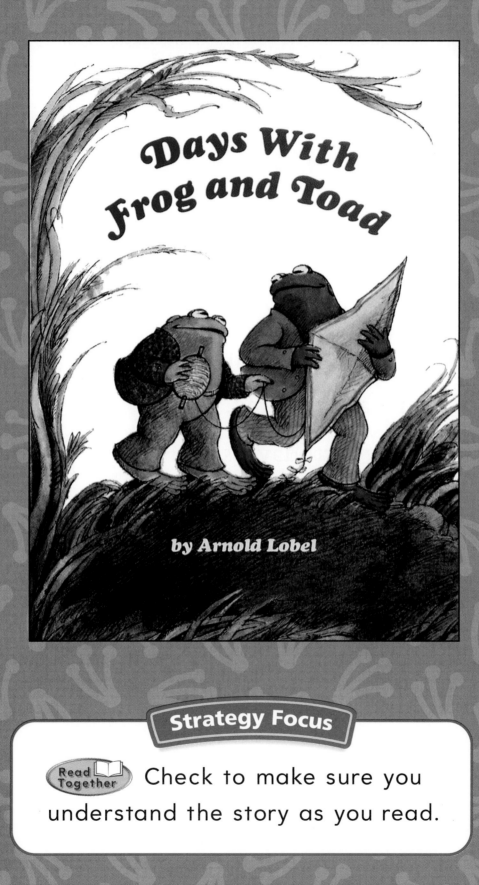

Days With
Frog and Toad

by Arnold Lobel

Strategy Focus

Read Together — Check to make sure you understand the story as you read.

The Hat

On Toad's birthday

Frog gave him a hat.

Toad was delighted.

"Happy birthday," said Frog.

Toad put on the hat.

It fell down over his eyes.

"I am sorry," said Frog.

"That hat is much too big for you.

I will give you something else."

"No," said Toad. "This hat
is your present to me. I like it.
I will wear it the way it is."

Frog and Toad went for a walk.

Toad tripped over a rock.

He bumped into a tree.

He fell in a hole.

"Frog," said Toad,

"I can't see anything.

I will not be able to wear

your beautiful present.

This is a sad birthday for me."

Frog and Toad
were sad
for a while.
Then Frog said,
"Toad, here is what you must do.
Tonight when you go to bed
you must think
some very big thoughts.
Those big thoughts will make
your head grow larger.
In the morning
your new hat may fit."
"What a good idea," said Toad.

That night when Toad went to bed
he thought the biggest thoughts
that he could think.
Toad thought about
giant sunflowers.
He thought about tall oak trees.
He thought about high mountains
covered with snow.

Then Toad fell asleep.

Frog came into Toad's house.

He came in quietly.

Frog found the hat
and took it to his house.

Frog poured some water on the hat.

He put the hat

in a warm place to dry.

It began to shrink.

That hat grew smaller and smaller.

Frog went back to Toad's house.

Toad was still fast asleep.

Frog put the hat back on the hook
where he found it.

When Toad woke up in the morning,
he put the hat on his head.

It was just the right size.

Toad ran to Frog's house.

"Frog, Frog!" he cried.

"All those big thoughts

have made my head

much larger.

Now I can wear your present!"

Frog and Toad went for a walk.

Toad did not trip

over a rock.

He did not bump into a tree.

He did not fall

in a hole.

It turned out to be

a very pleasant

day after Toad's birthday.

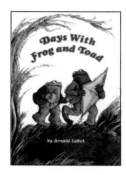

Think About the Story

1. How do you know that Frog and Toad were good friends?

2. What did Frog and Toad learn in this story?

3. What would you do with a hat that would not fit?

4. Were Frog and Toad the same kind of friends the bears were in *Two Greedy Bears*?

Internet

Complete a Web Crossword Puzzle

Use words from "The Hat" to complete a crossword puzzle. Print out the puzzle from Education Place.

www.eduplace.com/kids

What Shrinks?

Work with a small group to list some things that shrink. Why do you think they shrink?

Saying Thank You

Work with a partner. Take turns being Frog and Toad. Have a conversation in which Toad thanks Frog for the birthday present.

Evaluating

Write a Book Report

Write a book report and tell what you thought of the story.

Tips

- Include the title and author.
- Write complete sentences.

Skill: How to Read a Chart

- **Read** the headings.

- **Read** each set of facts.

- **Compare** the information.

- **Think** about what is alike and different about the facts.

Is It a Frog Or a Toad?

How can you tell the difference between a frog and a toad? Read the chart and look at the pictures.

Frogs	Toads
• Smooth, soft skin	• Thick, bumpy skin
• Long ridges down each side of back	• Short ridges on top of head
• Slender body, long legs, speedy swimmer	• Plump body, shorter legs, slower moving
• Lives in or very near water	• Lives on land, in woods
• Clumps of eggs laid in water	• Rows of eggs laid in water

Think about what you now know about frogs and toads. Look at the pictures. Can you tell which animals are frogs and which are toads?

1

2

3

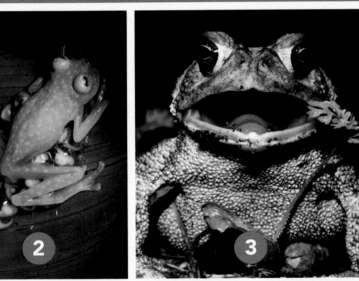

4

5

Frogs: 1, 2, 5
Toads: 3, 4

Writing a Personal Narrative

A test may ask you to write about something that really happened to you. Read this sample test.

> Write about a time when you got a birthday present for a friend. What happened?

Here is one student's plan.

What time will I write about?

Getting a present for Zach

Beginning

who the present was for

Details

what the present looked like

Tips

- **Read the test carefully. Look for key words that tell you what to write about.**

- **Make a plan before you write.**

- **After you finish writing, read your story. Correct any mistakes you see.**

Here is the student's answer.

The beginning tells what the narrative is about.

Zach's Present

I wanted to get my friend Zach a birthday present. I wanted to get him a bug book. Mom and I found the best book. It told about bugs and had big bug eyes that popped out on every page. Zach liked his book. That made me happy!

The writer uses the words *I* and *my*.

Details help the reader picture what happened.

The ending tells how the writer felt.

Glossary

A

appear

To **appear** means to come into view. The train will **appear** in five minutes.

appetite

Appetite means wanting food. I have a big **appetite** after I play.

argued

If you **argue** with someone, you don't agree. My brother and I **argued** about who would ride the bike.

B

beacon

A **beacon** is a light that warns people of danger. You can see the lighthouse **beacon** from miles away.

beautiful

Beautiful means very nice to look at or hear. Look at that **beautiful** painting on the wall.

bigger

Bigger means larger. That bus is **bigger** than our car.

birthday

Your **birthday** is the day you were born. We always give my mother gifts on her **birthday**.

built

To **build** is to make something. The work crew **built** a house with bricks.

C

canoe

A **canoe** is a long, thin boat. Ming used a paddle to steer the **canoe**.

cards

A **card** is a small piece of thick paper. We played a game with the **cards**.

cedar

A **cedar** is a kind of tree. We sat in the shade of the big **cedar** tree.

chicken

A **chicken** is a kind of bird. There were many **chickens** at the farm.

city

A **city** is a place where many people live and work. You can ride a bus or the subway in the **city**.

cookies

A **cookie** is a kind of food. May likes to have milk and **cookies**.

D

danger

Danger is something that can hurt you. An earthquake can put people in **danger**.

delighted

To be **delighted** means to be very happy about something. My father was **delighted** with his birthday present.

E

empty
Empty means with nothing inside. Todd drank his milk until his glass was **empty**.

equal
Equal means the same in amount or size. My father cut the sandwich into two **equal** pieces.

expected
To **expect** is to think something will happen. We **expected** the bus to be on time, but it was late.

F

favorite
Favorite means what you like the most. Spring is my **favorite** season of the year.

feathers
A **feather** is part of a bird. Most birds are covered with **feathers**.

field

A **field** is a big, flat piece of land without trees. The farmer grows hay in his **field**.

G

gathered

To **gather** means to put together. Nora **gathered** her books and put them into her backpack.

giant

Giant means much bigger than usual. The **giant** trees seemed to touch the sky.

gizzard

A **gizzard** is part of a bird's body. A bird's **gizzard** helps it break down the food it eats.

Grandaddy

Grandaddy is another name for grandfather. My **grandaddy** is my mother's father.

H

hungrier

To be **hungry** is to want to eat. I am always **hungrier** than my brother.

I

imagine

To **imagine** is to see a picture in your mind. On cold winter days, Kay likes to **imagine** that it is summer.

J

journey

A **journey** is a time when you travel somewhere. The **journey** through the mountains took many days.

L

larger

Large means big. A horse is **larger** than a dog.

M

mind

To **mind** is to care about something.
I don't **mind** if you borrow my crayons.

monarch

A **monarch** can be a kind of butterfly.
The **monarch** butterfly had beautiful
black and orange wings.

P

party

A **party** is a time when people
get together to have fun. All
my friends and family came to
my birthday **party**.

pleasant

Something that is **pleasant** makes you feel
happy. John and Rachel had a **pleasant**
day at the beach.

promises

To **promise** is to say you will do something.
Jill **promises** to be quiet during the movie.

R

remember

To **remember** is to be able to find something in your mind. Megan can **remember** all the names of the states.

S

seventh

Seventh means the one that is number seven. Anita was the **seventh** one in line.

smaller

Smaller is the opposite of bigger. A mouse is **smaller** than a horse.

soccer

Soccer is a sport you play by kicking a ball. In **soccer**, you try to kick a ball into a goal.

sorry

To be **sorry** is to feel sad about something. Luis was **sorry** that his friend couldn't sleep over.

stomach ache

A **stomach ache** is a pain in the belly.
Keith didn't go to school because he had
a **stomach ache**.

T

taught

To **teach** is to show how to do something.
My sister **taught** me how to ride a bike.

thirstier

To be **thirsty** is to need a drink. The hot
sun made me **thirstier**.

tired

To be **tired** is to feel weak and need rest.
The long hike made Jim very **tired**.

V

vacuum cleaner

A **vacuum cleaner** is a machine
that picks up dirt. I used the
vacuum cleaner to clean the rug.

W

warns

To **warn** is to let someone know about danger. The reporter **warns** us if a big storm is coming.

whispers

To **whisper** is to speak in a soft voice. My mother **whispers** to me when my baby brother is asleep.

Y

years

A **year** is 365 days. Ted is seven **years** old.

Acknowledgments

For each of the selections listed below, grateful acknowledgment is made for permission to excerpt and/or reprint original or copyrighted material, as follows:

Selections

Fireflies for Nathan, text by Shulamith Levey Oppenheim, illustrated by John Ward. Text copyright © 1994 by Shulamith Levey Oppenheim. Illustrations copyright © 1994 by John Ward. Reprinted by permission of HarperCollins Publishers.

Selection from *Fraction Action,* by Loreen Leedy. Copyright © 1994 by Loreen Leedy. All rights reserved. Reprinted by permission of Holiday House, Inc.

"The Hat" from *Days with Frog and Toad,* by Arnold Lobel. Copyright © 1979 by Arnold Lobel. Reprinted by permission of HarperCollins Publishers.

The New Friend, originally published as *El Amigo Nuevo,* by María Puncel, illustrations by Ulises Wensell. Copyright © 1995 by Laredo Publishing Company, Inc. Reprinted by permission of the publisher.

"Sister Hen's Cool Drink," retold by Angela Shelf Medearis in *A Bag of Tricks: Folk Tales from Around the World. Scholastic Phonics Chapter Books.* Copyright © 1998 by Scholastic, Inc. Reprinted by permission. Scholastic Phonics Chapter Books is a trademark of Scholastic, Inc.

The Surprise Family, by Lynn Reiser. Copyright © 1994 by Lynn Reiser. Reprinted by permission of HarperCollins Publishers.

Two Greedy Bears, by Mirra Ginsburg, illustrated by Jose Aruego and Ariane Dewey. Text copyright © 1976 by Mirra Ginsburg. Illustrations copyright © 1976 by Jose Aruego and Ariane Dewey. Reprinted with permission of Simon & Schuster Books for Young Readers, an imprint of Simon & Schuster Children's Publishing Division.

Selection from *Watch Them Grow,* by Linda Martin. Copyright © 1994 by Dorling Kindersley Limited, London. Text copyright © 1994 by Linda Martin. Reprinted by permission from Dorling Kindersley Publishing, Inc.

"What Is in Mole's Sack?" from *Meet Tricky Coyote!,* by Gretchen Will Mayo. Copyright © 1993 by Gretchen Will Mayo. Reprinted by permission of Walker Publishing.

When I Am Old with You, by Angela Johnson, illustrations by David Soman. Text copyright ©1990 by Angela Johnson. Illustrations copyright © 1990 by David Soman. Reprinted by permission of Orchard Books, New York.

Poetry

"A Year Later" from *The Llama Who Had No Pajama: 100 Favorite Poems,* by Mary Ann Hoberman. Copyright © 1959 by Mary Ann and Norman Hoberman. Reprinted with permission of Harcourt Inc.

"The Firefly" from *Beast Feast,* by Douglas Florian. Copyright © 1994 by Douglas Florian. Reprinted by permission of Harcourt Inc.

"Hope" from *Collected Poems,* by Langston Hughes. Copyright © 1994 by the Estate of Langston Hughes. Reprinted by permission of Alfred A. Knopf, a division of Random House, Inc.

"I'll walk halfway to your house" from *Halfway to Your House,* by Charlotte Pomerantz. Text copyright © 1993 by Charlotte Pomerantz. Reprinted by permission of HarperCollins Publishers.

"The New Girl" from *Everything Glistens and Everything Sings: New and Selected Poems,* by Charlotte Zolotow. Copyright © 1987 by Charlotte Zolotow. Reprinted with permission of Harcourt Inc.

Special thanks to the following teachers whose students' compositions appear as Student Writing Models: Cheryl Claxton, Florida; Patricia Kopay, Delaware; Susana Llanes, Michigan; Joan Rubens, Delaware; Nancy Schulten, Kentucky; Linda Wallis, California

Credits

Photography

3 (t) The Stock Market Royalty Free. **10** image Copyright © 2000 PhotoDisc, Inc. **12** (bkgd) Corbis Royalty Free. (icon) The Stock Market Royalty Free. **12–13** Lori Adamski Peek/Tony Stone Images. **14** Image Farm. **15** (frames) Image Farm. (l) image Copyright © 2000 PhotoDisc, Inc. (m) Jose Luis Pelaez/The Stock Market. (r) EyeWire. **44** (b) image Copyright © 2000 PhotoDisc, Inc. **45** (l) StockByte. (b) image Copyright © 2000 PhotoDisc, Inc. **46** (tl) Comstock KLIPS. (m) image Copyright © 2000 PhotoDisc, Inc. (b) Artville. **47** (tl) (tr) image Copyright © 2000 PhotoDisc, Inc. (bl) Artville. (br) Comstock KLIPS. **49** (t) image Copyright © 2000 PhotoDisc, Inc. **52** (m) Mike Tamborrino/Mercury Pictures. (b) Comstock KLIPS. **72** Comstock KLIPS. **76** (l) Image Farm/PictureQuest. **77** Robert P. Comport/Animals Animals. **78** (bkgd) Image Farm/PictureQuest. **109** Courtesy William Morrow. **138** (bkgd) Daizukan/Photonica. **141** Corbis Royalty Free. **142** Courtesy Mirra Ginsberg. **165** Tom Ianuzzi/Mercury Pictures. **172** Corbis Royalty Free. **200** Courtesy Shulamith Levey Oppenheim. **201** Tom Sciacca. **207** (t) (bl) StockByte. (mt) (mb) (br) images Copyright © 2000 PhotoDisc, Inc. **208** (t) Van Williams. (b) image Copyright © 2000 PhotoDisc, Inc. **222** (l) Randy Ury/The Stock Market. (r) Corbis/Susan Middleton & David Liittschwager. **223** (tr) Telegraph Colour Library/FPG International. (br) Stephen Dalton/Animals/Animals. (bl) Corbis/Lynda Richardson. (ml) Corbis/Michael & Patricia Fogden. (m) Corbis/Joe McDonald. **227** Comstock KLIPS. **228** image Copyright ©2000 PhotoDisc, Inc. **229** image Copyright ©2000 PhotoDisc, Inc. **230** image Copyright ©2000 PhotoDisc, Inc. **231** image Copyright ©2000 PhotoDisc, Inc. **232** image Copyright ©2000 PhotoDisc, Inc. **233** Lori Adamski Peek/Tony Stone Images. **234** Corbis Royalty Free. **235** image Copyright ©2000 PhotoDisc, Inc.

Assignment Photography

44 (t) Allen Landau. **45** (r), **46** (tr), **51, 73** (t), **117, 225** Tony Scarpetta. **138–9, 143** (bkgd), **175, 203, 221** Joel Benjamin.

Illustration

53–71 Ed Martinez. **74–75** David Diaz. **78** (i), **79–109** Lynn Reiser. **118–119** Normand Cousineau. **120–127** Bob Barner. **128–135** Gerardo Suzan. **204–205** Laura Huliska-Beith. **206** (tr), **209** (i), **210–219** Arnold Lobel.